the URBAN ANIMAL

BY
BARBARA TAYLOR

CHEVROLET

Ne jamais écrire
dans les documents

ALASKA '91
3890 CR

D0316271

LIVING ON THE WILD SIDE

Flocks of pigeons fluttering in your face in a city center; the eyes of a fox shining in car headlights; the sound of a mouse scurrying around under the floorboards – three familiar examples of the wild animals that share our urban environment. And there are many more. Some are visible, many are hidden out of sight, but they all take advantage of the benefits of urban living, such as food all year around, warmer temperatures in winter months, and a variety of places to shelter and nest. Urban animals have to be adaptable and able to survive constant change, noise, lights, pollution, and disturbance from hordes of people and traffic. Those wild animals that have adapted to the challenges of urban living sometimes exist in large numbers, often becoming pests or health hazards.

HIGH-RISE NESTS

White storks normally nest in tall trees, but chimneys, spires, and pylons are a good substitute. In some European towns, people have built special platforms on their chimneys to act as a base for the huge mass of sticks and other nesting materials that the storks use. The storks are supposed to bring good fortune and many children to those people lucky enough to have a nest on their roof, although the storks themselves have not been so lucky and numbers have been falling.

CATS GONE WILD

In many cities there are staggering populations of feral cats. These are domestic cats that have been abandoned or made homeless because of war, fire, or floods. Feral cats are independent, secretive, and nocturnal, living in factories, warehouses, sewers, and docklands. They hunt birds, rats, and mice. Without them, the problem of urban rats and mice would be more serious.

NESTING SITES

Swallows, swifts, and house martins were originally cave or cliff dwellers that now nest on or in buildings. A swallow's nest is usually supported by a rafter, shelf, or ledge. The saucer-shaped nest is made from mud and dried grasses, lined with feathers and bits of plants. Swallows also rest on artificial perches, such as telegraph poles and wires, rather than natural perches, such as trees.

SUPER SURVIVORS

Rats and mice thrive in the heart of the largest and dirtiest cities all over the world. Thousands of brown rats like this one live beneath our feet in sewers, drains, and other underground tunnels. Black rats originally lived in trees and like to climb. They make their home aboveground in roof and attic spaces. Rats and mice first spread to urban habitats by traveling on ships from one port to another.

POPULAR PIGEONS?

Like swallows, pigeons are rock and cliff-dwelling birds that now make their homes on the artificial cliffs of our cities. One of the reasons for their spectacular success as an urban animal is that they can breed all year round. Some people like the pigeons so much that they feed them – although not always from their own mouths! In Roman times, pigeons were so highly regarded that slaves had to chew bread before it was given to the pigeons. Today, they cause many problems in towns because of the mess they make and the diseases they carry.

ROAD SAFETY

Deciding when to cross a road is a terrifying prospect for many urban animals. Common toads set off to find their breeding ponds in spring but often find their migration route blocked by paved highways.

NORTH & SOUTH AMERICAN CITIES

From the cold, snowy wastes of Canada to the tropical warmth of Florida or Brazil, a surprising variety of wild animals have made their homes in American cities. Polar bears scavenge around garbage dumps in sub-Arctic Canadian towns, while moose sometimes leave the forests and wander through the streets. Peregrine falcons nest on skyscrapers in Los Angeles, swifts nest in chimneys instead of hollow trees, caimans live in the canal systems of Florida, and raccoons are common where there is plenty of garbage. In some South American cities, house mice with very thick fur even survive in refrigerated warehouses. But American cities also have plenty of the most common city birds – the house sparrow, the feral pigeon, and the starling. They are not native birds but were introduced at different times – pigeons in the 17th century, sparrows between 1850 and 1870, and starlings in 1890–1891, when a flock of 100 birds were released into Central Park, New York. Today, there are over 50 million in North America.

GARDEN PEST

Rabbits such as this eastern cottontail rabbit have become pests in some parts of America, eating away at garden plants and digging up the flowerbeds. They are difficult to catch because their large, mobile ears help them to detect danger, and their long legs are adapted for fast running. They are good at burrowing and gnawing and often find a way through rabbit-proof fencing.

SUNBATHING SLOTH

In a city park in Santa Cruz, Bolivia, lives a colony of sloths. This one seems to be enjoying the sunshine since sloths regulate their body temperature by moving in and out of the sun. It is not frightened of being so close to people. When wild animals are fed regularly by people, they can become very tame.

HAPPY HUMMERS

Hummingbirds have no fear of people so they have no problem living in cities. People in North America often hang hummingbird feeders in their back yards because they enjoy watching the tiny birds. Inside the feeders is a sugary liquid, rather like the nectar hummingbirds take from flowers. Sugar is a good food for hummingbirds because it can be turned into energy very quickly and hummingbirds need a lot of instant energy to keep their tiny bodies warm.

DEER LUNCH

Some wapiti deer seem to find these playing fields an ideal spot for a rest and a grassy lunch. Urban areas can provide deer with safe refuges from hunters, although such large mammals are not common in towns.

PEREGRINE PERCHES

City centers are ideal for peregrine falcons because the tall buildings are just like the rocky cliffs on which they like to breed. There are also plenty of pigeons to eat. In the U.S., many young birds bred in captivity have been introduced to cities such as Washington, Baltimore, Cincinnati, Cleveland, and Los Angeles. Humans act as surrogate parents, supervising and feeding the birds until they can look after themselves. About a dozen chicks need to be released over two years to ensure one breeding pair. Dangers such as plate-glass windows and wires cause the death of eight out of ten of the young birds.

SKUNK STINK

In American towns, skunks often live in graveyards, emerging after dusk to scavenge for food. A skunk's bold black-and-white stripes carry a warning that no one can afford to ignore. To defend itself, a skunk squirts out a terrible smelling, amber-colored fluid from its anal glands. Anyone who gets this on their clothes while trying to chase a skunk off their property might as well throw their clothes away, although tomato juice is supposed to reduce the time that the smell lasts.

SPINY VISITOR

A hedgehog finds a suburban garden very similar to its natural habitat of woodland edges. It has the same sort of food, such as worms, slugs, snails, beetles, and caterpillars, as well as leaves and grasses for nesting material. Unfortunately, there are a lot of hazards for city hedgehogs. Slug pellets may become a poisoned snack; ponds with smooth sides may be impossible to climb out of; and autumn bonfires may accidentally be started on top of hibernating hedgehogs.

FEATHERED HUNTERS

Owls, such as the ghostly white barn owl (left), the tawny owl, and the little owl, take advantage of the many rodents scurrying about towns, offering them an easy meal. Barn owls have even nested in the belfry of the cathedral of Notre Dame in Paris. The snoring and hissing of barn owl fledglings in church towers may have been partly responsible for stories of ghosts and goblins roaming about the churchyards at night.

BUTTERFLY BONANZA

The butterfly bush, *Buddleja davidii*, was introduced from China to Europe and North America as a garden shrub about 100 years ago. Now it thrives on town building sites and wasteland, as well as in town gardens. Its flowers are extremely attractive to 20 or more species of butterfly, such as these peacocks, as well as other nectar-feeding insects, such as hoverflies and bumble bees.

EUROPEAN CITIES

Europe is a busy place. In many European countries, large numbers of people are crowded into noisy towns and cities. The European climate is generally temperate, becoming icy cold in the far north and warmer in the south. Elk have wandered into snowy Moscow, not very far from Red Square, yet in some towns in southern France, the buzzing of semi-tropical cicadas fills the air. Some urban animals have spread eastward from Europe to other parts of the world, for instance rabbits and starlings have spread to Australia. Others have moved in the opposite direction – collared doves spread across Europe from Istanbul and brown rats traveled west from their haunts in Russia. European scavengers, such as kites and ravens, have all but disappeared as sanitary conditions have improved. There is, however, still one famous band of ravens kept at the Tower of London.

PIGEON ESCAPES

The hordes of feral pigeons that are at home in all cities, from London's Trafalgar Square to the Blue Mosque in Afghanistan, are the descendants of domesticated birds reared as a source of food.

They were first domesticated in Iraq over 6,000 years ago. Some city pigeons may also have come from racing pigeons that strayed or became lost. Feral pigeons are remarkably variable in color and markings, due partly to breeding and partly as an adaptation to the town environment. Dark colored birds may survive better in colder climates, as dark colors absorb the sun's warmth. Lighter colored birds stay cooler in warmer climates as light colors reflect the heat.

GREY INVADERS

The grey squirrel is a North American species that was introduced to Britain at the turn of the century to give the local gentry something to shoot. About 30 additional introductions followed, leading to a population explosion of grey squirrels and the gradual decline of its red cousin. Grey squirrels love to chew and can cause serious problems if they nest in attic spaces or get inside houses.

ASIAN &
AUSTRALIAN CITIES

SCARY SPIDERS

The Sydney funnel-web spider is one of the most dangerous spiders in the world. They live in an area about 100 miles (160 km) from the center of Sydney. Females rarely move far from their burrows but may bite people while they are gardening or gathering logs. Males sometimes enter houses in summer when searching for females and may crawl into shoes or clothing left on the floor. Both sexes are very aggressive and their massive fangs can go through a child's fingernail.

The urban animals of southern Asia and Australia are drawn to the cities by the opportunities for shelter and the excellent supplies of food. In India, certain animals, such as cows and monkeys, are venerated and protected for religious reasons, while jackals, vultures, and kites scavenge for leftovers. Some house guests, such as the house gecko, are welcome for clearing the rooms of insect pests. Geckos are also considered lucky animals. Others, such as deadly poisonous spiders or snakes, are widely feared. Australian city wildlife is dominated by marsupials, such as possums nesting in attics. There are also a number of urban species that were introduced to Australia from Europe, such as starlings, sparrows, and rabbits. In turn, foxes, stoats, and weasels were introduced in the 19th century to combat a rabbit plague. They were unsuccessful but are still living in Australia today.

TEMPLE MONKEYS

Monkeys, such as these sitting on the Monkey Temple in Nepal, are treated well by Hindus because of the Hindu monkey god, Hanuman. In the Sanskrit epic, the Ramayana, dating from about 3300 B.C., the monkey chieftain Hanuman helps Rama (an incarnation of the god Vishnu) to recover his wife who has been abducted by demon king Ravana. There are probably more monkeys living in the cities in India than in the forests.

POSSUM LODGERS

In Australian cities, such as
Sydney and Melbourne,
cat-sized common brushtail
possums have invaded homes in considerable
numbers. This mother and young are nesting in a
boarded-up chimney. They also get into attics,
where they sometimes rip up ceilings to set up home.
These possums also raid garbage cans and bird feeders
in suburban gardens.

SACRED COWS

Cows like this are allowed
to wander freely through the
streets of Indian cities and
even raid vegetable stalls.
Hindus respect animal life
and believe that when we
hurt living things, we hurt
ourselves. Many Hindus are
vegetarians. They also think
of cows, which give people
milk to drink, as mothers,
and they never eat beef.

MEGABATS

Fruit bats have furry, fox-like faces and so are also called flying foxes.
They roost in trees during the day; sometimes stripping away leaves so
the members of the colony can see each other more clearly. At dusk
they leave their roosts in search of food. In cities such as
Sydney, they feed on the fig trees in the city parks
at night and can often be heard making
harsh, squealing noises.

STREETWISE
KANGAROO

Hopping along a
street in Queensland,
Australia, are a mother
and joey (baby) eastern
grey kangaroo. The mother
has only one young at a time
and the young leave the pouch when
they are about 10 months old. Since the late 18th century,
human settlement has brought dramatic changes to the kangaroo's
original habitat, forcing them to compete for grazing land and cope
with predators, such as domestic cats, dogs, and European red foxes.

AFRICAN CITIES

Temperatures in African cities are generally high, night and day, except in a few mountainous areas. Rainfall varies a good deal, from the dry, arid northern cities, such as Cairo, to the wet, lush southern cities, such as Cape Town. European starlings were first introduced into Africa in Cape Town, supposedly by Cecil Rhodes, the 19th century South African statesman. Since then, they have rapidly extended their range. There are also tropical birds, such as weaverbirds, scavenging for leftovers and sunbirds flitting about parks and gardens. Geckos fulfill a useful role eating insects in buildings, but one, the lobe-footed gecko, used to be regarded with unnecessary dread in Egyptian towns and named "the father of leprosy." Termites can also be bad news because of the damage they cause to wooden buildings. African city mammals include rats and monkeys, which can be a considerable nuisance.

TAME BIRD

The African pied wagtail is a very tame and confiding bird that is closely associated with human dwellings. It lives in pairs or small parties and has a pleasant warbling song rather like that of a canary.

This wagtail nests in holes in buildings and riverbanks, laying three eggs with many pale, yellowish-brown markings.

CAMP FOLLOWER

This African elephant has wandered into a tourist camp in the Masai Mara National Park in Kenya. Elephants are intelligent animals and they soon learn that human camps are useful sources of extra food or water. Sometimes, camps are built across traditional migration routes of elephants. Because they are such huge animals, they are difficult to keep out of the camps and may cause damage with their huge bulk. But for the tourists, the chance to get really close to a wild elephant is an amazing experience. Other game animals can also get too close for comfort. In 1898–1899 the man-eating lions of Tsavo stopped all work on the Mombasa to Uganda railroad when workers refused to continue until they were protected. The two lions killed 135 men before they were finally shot.

ROOFTOP MONKEYS

Colobus monkeys are good climbers and jumpers – their long hairs and tails act as parachutes when they leap. In the forests, they rarely descend to the ground, so climbing onto this Kenyan rooftop must have been easy for them. They may be looking for leaves to eat in the garden around the house.

VULTURE DUTY

Stalking about with their characteristic goose step, Egyptian vultures search for morsels of food among the town and city garbage dumps of North, Central, and East Africa. These vultures also feed on human excrement. The Egyptian vulture is one of the few tool-using birds, breaking eggs by throwing stones onto them.

GAS STATION ATTENDANT

This yellow baboon looks as if it is waiting to serve a customer with gasoline. It may be waiting for a car to arrive in the hope of a free snack. This is a large, slender baboon, that reaches lengths of up to and over 3 ft (102 cm) without the tail and has conspicuously long legs. It comes out during the day and lives in groups.

THE ULTIMATE URBAN ANIMAL

R ed foxes are common worldwide. They are widespread and numerous in urban Britain, but also live in other cities of Europe, Australia, and North America. Foxes have adapted well to city living because they are not very fussy about where they live or what they eat. They are small enough to be unobtrusive, yet large enough to travel long distances in search of food. Some foxes are commuters, only coming into town at night to eat. Urban areas provide foxes with refuge from hunters and traps. Other urban members of the dog family include dingoes, jackals, and coyotes.

AMERICAN FOXES

This red fox has set up home in a Colorado cemetery. In North America, urban red foxes have to compete with raccoons, coyotes, bobcats, and even cougars. They have not become such familiar urban animals as they have in countries such as Britain.

Adult foxes molt their fur once each year, between spring and midsummer. While molting, they often look scruffy, thin and long legged. In winter, they grow thick, warm coats.

Most urban foxes lead short lives – 55 percent die in their first year and 80 percent die before they are three years old. A few dominant, and lucky, animals may survive to live and breed for up to eight years.

Foxes have keen hearing to detect the rustling noises made by voles and other rodents as they move.

Touch-sensitive whiskers and hairs on the muzzle, around the eyes, and under the chin help the fox to find its way through vegetation or explore new runs or holes.

Foxes have 42 teeth, including four sharp, pointed canines to kill and tear prey and carnassial teeth in the side of the mouth for cutting food.

Foxes are relatively small animals, only a little heavier than a pet cat.

FOX SPEAK

To most city dwellers, it is the eerie, blood-chilling screams of foxes in the middle of the night that are most familiar.

It is generally the vixens (females) that scream, while the dog foxes bark. These strange noises can be heard at any time of year but are more common in January, when foxes are dispersing and mating.

TRACKING FOXES

To build up a picture of the number of foxes in towns and cities and how they move about, scientists study their tracks and droppings.

FOX: FRONT FOOT   **FOX: BACK FOOT**   **DOG**

Fox footprints are like those of a small dog, only narrower. Claw marks are usually clearly visible.

FRESH (DARK)

DRY (WHITE)

Fox droppings are about 2¼–4 in (7–10cm) long. They look like dog droppings but have a twisted point at one end. They are usually dark and may be made up of bits of mice, birds, hard parts of insects, fruit, and berries. Older droppings become paler and much more brittle.

DINGO DOGS

The original dingo was a primitive dog that is probably descended from the Indian wolf. It was spread through east Asia by traders and travelers and apparently arrived in Australia some 4,000–6,000 years ago. Today's dingoes breed freely with feral dogs and few pure dingo populations remain.

Dingoes scavenge on garbage heaps but have a wide and varied diet.

CITY COYOTE

In some of the western cites of the United States coyotes have adapted well to urban life. They are particularly common in Los Angeles, where they hide in scrub-filled ravines during the day and move into built-up areas to feed at night. Coyotes can breed with domestic dogs to produce "coydogs," which are more likely to attack domestic animals, such as cats, dogs, and chickens. Coyotes have even attacked people, which is one thing that urban foxes never do.

DAYTIME VISITORS

MOLE MOUNTAINS

Moles can make a real mess of a grassy lawn in a garden or town park and they are very difficult to get rid of. The molehills we see above ground are the waste soil that they push above ground as they dig their tunnels. Most of their food comes from soil animals, such as worms that fall into their tunnels. In places where food is scarce, moles have to dig more burrows and push up more molehills to find enough food to eat.

Different urban animals are active by day and by night. This helps them to share the resources of the urban habitat and avoid competition. Daytime creatures, such as squirrels, are the ones we are most likely to notice, although the night is usually a busier time because most of the people are out of the way. People are the biggest nuisance for urban animals. They swat houseflies, flick away the cobwebs of house spiders, and chase squirrels and wasps away from their picnics. The residents of Tokyo swatted about 117 million houseflies on National Fly Day in 1933. People also prevent larger animals from getting in the way of their daily lives, by building fences around their golf courses or culling populations if they become a problem. But one of the reasons that urban animals survive is that they are not easily frightened by people.

SUPERMARKET SHOPPER

This great egret has no intention of paying for its food at the checkout of this Florida supermarket. Instead, it has spotted a few meat scraps lying about and has moved in to claim a free meal. Great egrets usually feed in swamps and marshes, stalking fish, frogs, snakes, and crayfish in shallow water. As people have invaded its natural habitat, the great egret has been forced to change some of its feeding habits.

KANGAROO GOLFERS

These kangaroos have taken advantage of this empty Australian golf course to grab a tasty grass snack. It is difficult to make such areas kangaroo proof as kangaroos are good at jumping fences and can leap 9.5 ft (3 meters) in height and 29.5 ft (9 meters) in length. Normally, kangaroos graze during the night and rest up in the shade during the day.

FREE FOOD

Grey squirrels will eat almost anything, from garden bulbs, fish, honey, and fruit to fungi, carrion, and young birds and their eggs. They take full advantage of any free meals people leave out for them. Grey squirrels are agile and alert animals with a good sense of smell and very good eyesight. They spend a good deal of time foraging on the ground and have to be always ready to spring into the trees at the first sign of danger.

STRIPED ANGEL

People are usually afraid of wasps, because they can sting, but they are in fact very beneficial insects. For most of the summer they hunt insect pests in the garden and are far too busy getting food for their young to bother us. At the end of the summer, a wasp colony starts to break up. The workers have no more young to feed and start to turn their attention to fruit and other sweet substances. This is when the wasps can be annoying, but as soon as the weather turns cold, they die. Only the mated queens survive the winter.

A NIGHT ON THE TOWN

A s the sun sets and people settle down inside their homes for the night, a whole new shift of animals emerges from their daytime hiding places. Animal sounds are easier to hear at night because there is less traffic – the hoot of an owl, the snuffling of a badger, the rustling of a raccoon, the fluttering of a moth, or the scream of a fox. Many small animals find it easier to hide from their enemies in the darkness. Nighttime animals have keen senses, especially of hearing and smell, to help them search for food or mates or detect danger. Animals that lose water easily, such as slugs, snails, and woodlice, prefer to come out at night because the air is cooler and damper. In some countries in the spring, a striking dawn chorus ends the night, as the birds all sing to lay claim to their nesting territory.

BADGER VISIT

Badgers often visit towns for food, but more because the town has spread into their bit of countryside rather than because they have moved into town. They need open space and peace and quiet and are not as adaptable as many urban animals, except in their diet. Badgers eat many things. They love earthworms but will also eat carrion, insects, small mammals and birds, fruit, vegetables, and seeds. They have even been seen crunching glass bottles and chewing golf balls.

SUPER MICE

House mice can live almost anywhere – in coal mines, subway stations, or even refrigerated warehouses. They have good eyesight and a particularly good sense of smell. They can also run fast, which is possibly the best defense against their biggest predator – the cat. House mice usually live in extended families with a dominant male, his harem of females, and several generations of their offspring. One female mouse can have about 25 young in a year. As well as eating our food, house mice can be a problem because they spread diseases and even set off burglar alarms as they patter around the house at night.

CITIZEN RACCOON

The streetwise raccoon not only tolerates people but seems to thrive in dense human settlements such as towns and cities in North America. Generally shy by nature, raccoons time their visits for the hours when humans are fewer, garbage is fresher, and bird feeders are fully stocked. They may build their dens in chimneys or drains, which are like the hollow branches or tree trunks in which they nest in the wild. Raccoons succeed at urban life because they are secretive, adaptable, and able to make a meal out of most natural and artificial city foodstuffs. A city can also be a refuge for raccoons, as they may be trapped and hunted in the countryside.

TOAD TRAVELER

In 1935, some 62,000 South American cane toads were released into Queensland, Australia in an attempt to control sugarcane pests. The toads spread to many other areas, including residential ones, and began to eat useful creatures, such as mice, geckos, and small frogs. Cane toads have proved rather too successful since they eat almost anything, produce vast numbers of eggs (up to 30,000 eggs per clutch), and do not have any serious predators in Australia. At night they can often be seen sitting under streetlights or garden lights, plucking flying insects out of the air.

BATTY SUPERSTITIONS

Despite their image of mystery and sinister happenings, bats are in fact unobtrusive and inoffensive animals that are anxious to avoid their human neighbors. They prefer to roost in modern, clean houses rather than dusty, drafty old ones. They are scrupulously clean and usually quiet and nonsmelly. Long-eared bats like these have the longest ears relative to their body size of any mammal. They use their sensitive ears to pick up the echoes of high-pitched sounds they make. This is called "echolocation" and helps most bats to navigate and find food.

LUCKY GECKOS

In tropical countries, the sound of a gecko in the bedroom at night is a welcome one because it is there to catch insects. Geckos are the only reptiles with a true voice. In Bangkok, it is supposed to be an especially good sign if a gecko happens to be uttering its cry when a baby is born. Geckos have a kind of suction pad under their toes to help them scurry up and down the walls, and even upside down across the ceiling.

HOUSE PARTY

D id you know that about one million dust mites live in an ordinary single bed? Or that book lice feed on the tiny molds that grow on the pages of books or under wallpaper? These are just two of the many creatures that lurk unseen in the hidden corners of our homes – on walls, or in wardrobes, carpets, curtains, and kitchen cupboards. Many of them are tiny, or even microscopic, but a few, such as bats in the attic or mice under the floorboards, are larger, noisier, and more obvious. Some of them would once have lived in caves or big holes in trees but prefer the warmth of our homes, with their built-in food supply. The larvae of many moths and beetles munch their way through our food, clothes, curtains, and carpets. They include clothes moths, meal moths, flour beetles, bacon beetles, leather beetles, grain weevils, and carpet beetles. Some of these insects find their way into our homes from the nests of birds, rodents, and wasps, which are built in and around human habitations.

DUST FOR DINNER

Billions of microscopic dust mites chomp away on the bits of dead skin that flake off our bodies. Much of the dust in our homes is made up of human skin! Dust mites are so small you cannot see them and no one knew they were there until about 30 years ago. Some people are allergic to dust mite droppings. They sniffle and sneeze and even get asthma if they breathe in too many of them.

YUMMY CARPETS

Carpet beetle larvae are covered with hairs so are called woolly bears. They feed on woolen textiles, hair, feathers, and offal. Adult females lay their eggs in places where there will be food for the larvae. In the wild, the eggs are laid in the nests of mice and birds. Adult carpet beetles fly around outside during the summer and feed on nectar and pollen. They often find their way indoors.

Swallows and house martins may nest under the eaves of houses.

SWALLOWS

ANIMAL LODGERS

The artificial habitats in our homes are similar to many natural ones – walls are like cliffs, attics and cellars are like caves, chimneys are like tall trees, and wooden furniture is like the fallen logs in a forest. Even though we may not be aware of it, our homes are full of uninvited guests. Some can cause problems by carrying diseases or destroying the structure of our homes and the things in them. Others, such as spiders and geckos, are useful because they eat unwanted insects.

Bats are safe from predators in the attic. Young bats can practice flying there too.

BATS

STORKS

Wasps may build their paper nests from attic beams.

WASPS

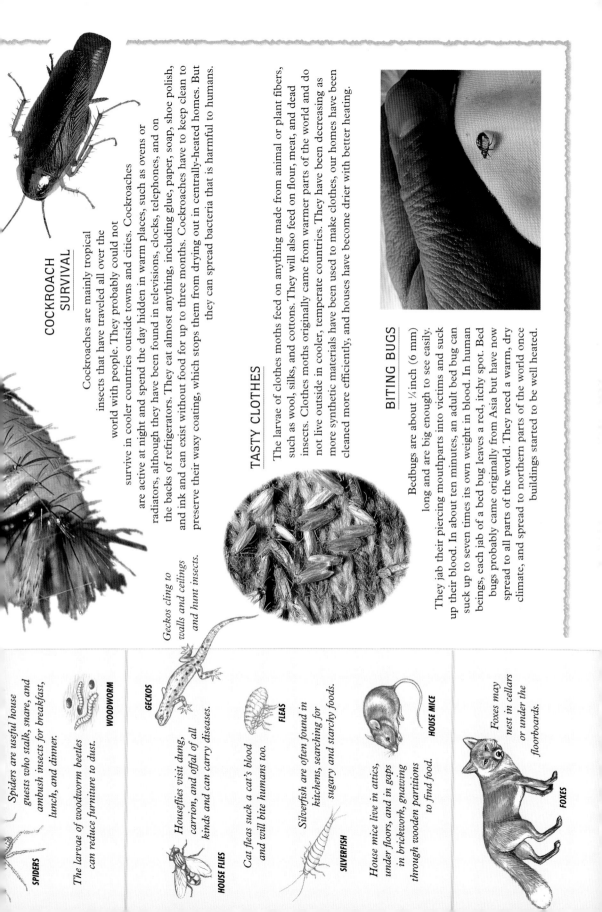

COCKROACH SURVIVAL

Cockroaches are mainly tropical insects that have traveled all over the world with people. They probably could not survive in cooler countries outside towns and cities. Cockroaches are active at night and spend the day hidden in warm places, such as ovens or radiators. They have been found in televisions, clocks, telephones, and on the backs of refrigerators. They eat almost anything, including glue, paper, soap, shoe polish, and ink and can exist without food for up to three months. Cockroaches have to keep clean to preserve their waxy coating, which stops them from drying out in centrally-heated homes. But they can spread bacteria that is harmful to humans.

TASTY CLOTHES

The larvae of clothes moths feed on anything made from animal or plant fibers, such as wool, silks, and cottons. They will also feed on flour, meat, and dead insects. Clothes moths originally came from warmer parts of the world and do not live outside in cooler, temperate countries. They have been decreasing as more synthetic materials have been used to make clothes, our homes have been cleaned more efficiently, and houses have become drier with better heating.

BITING BUGS

Bedbugs are about ¼ inch (6 mm) long and are big enough to see easily. They jab their piercing mouthparts into victims and suck up their blood. In about ten minutes, an adult bed bug can suck up to seven times its own weight in blood. In human beings, each jab of a bed bug leaves a red, itchy spot. Bed bugs probably came originally from Asia but have now spread to all parts of the world. They need a warm, dry climate, and spread to northern parts of the world once buildings started to be well heated.

Geckos cling to walls and ceilings and hunt insects.

SPIDERS

Spiders are useful house guests who stalk, snare, and ambush insects for breakfast, lunch, and dinner.

WOODWORM

The larvae of woodworm beetles can reduce furniture to dust.

GECKOS

FLEAS

Houseflies visit dung, carrion, and offal of all kinds and can carry diseases.

HOUSE FLIES

Cat fleas suck a cat's blood and will bite humans too.

SILVERFISH

Silverfish are often found in kitchens, searching for sugary and starchy foods.

HOUSE MICE

House mice live in attics, under floors, and in gaps in brickwork, gnawing through wooden partitions to find food.

FOXES

Foxes may nest in cellars or under the floorboards.

ON THE ROAD

T he roads that crisscross our towns and cities can be useful as corridors, allowing animals to disperse from one area to another. They can also provide feeding grounds for insects and small seed-eating birds as well as hunting birds, such as kestrels and owls, or scavengers such as crows, magpies, and jackdaws. But, on the whole, they are polluted and dangerous barriers to animals, especially slow-moving ones, such as toads, that need to cross roads to reach their breeding ponds, or low-flying birds, such as blackbirds. Badgers suffer badly, too, because roads may cut across the traditional tracks they follow from place to place. The usual defenses of many animals are useless against cars and trucks – hedgehogs roll up into a ball and rely on their spines for protection; deer and rabbits freeze if they think running is too risky. Sometimes animals are protected by people who set up special crossing points on roads.

LOOK-OUT POINT

A kestrel perches on a highway bridge, keeping a sharp lookout along the roadside embankments for small birds or rodents. Kestrels seem to be unconcerned by the traffic thundering along beneath them. They are the only birds that can truly hover in the air, keeping the head still to form a stable platform for the keen eyes. Close-cropped embankments where small animals have little chance to hide provide kestrels with good hunting.

ANIMAL CROSSINGS

Specially designed signs aim to draw drivers' attention to the possibility of animals on the road, rather like the warning signs showing children outside schools. The hope is that the drivers will slow down and take more care once they see the signs. People sometimes stand by the side of the road to help toads get across the roads safely as they migrate to their breeding grounds at night.

KOALA WALKABOUT

This koala has not chosen a good spot for watching the traffic. Although koalas spend much of their time in the trees, they often come to the ground where they can run nimbly. They are also excellent swimmers. Koalas usually occupy home ranges of about 7–10 acres (3–4 hectares) but journeys of 18 miles (30 km) or more have been recorded.

ROAD CASUALTIES

This fox is yet another victim of a speeding car. Snakes are often killed when they come out to lie on a warm road surface. Every driver is unfortunately familiar with the toll of animals seen flattened on the road or lying battered at the edge. Even if an animal is only injured, it may die later from the shock of the accident or be too badly injured to survive in the wild.

TURTLE VERSUS TRUCK

With an enormous truck speeding towards it only a few feet away, a slow-moving turtle has little chance of crossing the road safely. Its strong shell was not designed to withstand such a powerful crushing force. Semi-terrestrial turtles live both in water and on land and eat both plants and animal food.

THE CLEAN-UP CREWS

F rom household garbage left outside our homes to garbage left on the streets or dumped in large landfill sites, the food we throw away feeds a surprising variety of urban animals and winged scavengers. Bacterial decomposition of the garbage releases warmth and this attracts indoor scavengers, such as cockroaches and house crickets, as well as mice in the winter. Reptiles such as grass snakes, lizards, and slowworms may also exploit the internal warmth of a landfill site. The myriad of garbage-dwelling invertebrates (animals without a backbone) includes dung flies, bluebottles, houseflies, hoverflies, owl midges, spiders, bees, earth worms, roundworms, and springtails. All these creatures act as natural recyclers, making good use of the garbage we throw away.

GARBAGE RATS

Rats thrive in the dirtiest parts of town, which include landfill sites. Rats in the Italian city of Pisa were once deprived of their staple diet by the installation of a new garbage incinerator. They responded by swarming into the city center, only leaving when refuse was delivered from a neighboring town. Rats are intelligent, cunning survivors, but they cause immense damage in towns, as well as spreading diseases.

GREEDY GULLS

The harsh sound of gulls squabbling over juicy bits of refuse is a noisy reminder of the important role scavengers play in the natural world. These gulls have turned their back on the sea and now spend most of the year feeding at landfill sites instead. They migrate to the coast only to breed. The gulls are tough and aggressive and find rich pickings among the garbage. Some species even rob other gulls of their food. Common gulls get almost all of their own food by robbing black-headed gulls.

BEAR VISITORS

In the autumn, large numbers of polar bears pass by a town called Churchill, in Canada, on their way to reach their hunting grounds, far out over the frozen ice covering Hudson Bay. The bears are hungry after spending summer on land, where there are no seals for them to hunt. They find the garbage dump of Churchill particularly attractive. The bears are a serious hazard to the people of Churchill, however, since they are very strong and unpredictable.

RACCOON PROOF?

Raccoons are able to defeat most attempts to make garbage cans "raccoon proof," since they have dextrous front paws that can even unscrew lids or pull tops from bottles. They have been known to lift a door latch, walk into a kitchen, open a refrigerator, and help themselves to the contents.

SCAVENGER STORK

Marabou storks of Africa obtain most of their food by scavenging and are often attracted to human landfill sites. They need over 24 oz (700 g) of food each day and also scavenge at lion kills, where they compete with vultures and hyenas for food. Their size and large bills help them to steal bits of food from nearby vultures. Here they are joined by some baboons, hoping to find an easy meal.

WOOLLY RECYCLERS

People do throw away an awful lot of food, which makes a tasty free meal for many animals. These Welsh sheep may not be the most common visitors to garbage dumps but they are helping to recycle some of our garbage. This is useful as there is too much human garbage and not enough places for it to go. Garbage can contain sharp or broken objects though, which can injure both animals and people sorting through the leftovers.

URBAN WETLANDS

Even though many towns and cities are built near rivers and streams, it is often the artificial waterways of canals, reservoirs, old gravel pits, and park or garden ponds that are more useful for wildlife. Reservoirs are particularly important as wintering grounds for migrating wildfowl. Slow-moving canal waters shelter pond creatures, such as frogs, pond skaters, water voles, and moorhens. Bridges and other canal-side buildings provide roosting sites for bats. Ponds are fascinating mini-ecosystems for a variety of invertebrates, as well as frogs, newts, and fish. Larger animals such as foxes and hedgehogs may drink from them. Spectacular, jewel-like kingfishers are also sometimes glimpsed along waterways right in the middle of towns.

SPINNING BEETLES

On the surface of still or slow-flowing waters, shiny whirligig beetles spin gracefully in small groups. Most of their legs are flattened and fringed with hairs for swimming. The eyes are divided into two parts, the top part for seeing in the air and the bottom part for seeing under the water. Adult whirligig beetles feed mainly on insects that have fallen onto the surface of the water. To survive low winter temperatures, the whirligigs bury themselves in the mud.

SLOW MOVER

Unlike most water snails, which eat only plants, the great pond snail also eats decaying animals, fish eggs, and even small fish. It is common in large ponds in Britain and Europe and has also become established in Australia, Asia, and the middle states of the U.S. Great pond snails can obtain oxygen from the air using a simple lung and remain submerged for long periods in well-oxygenated waters.

MOSQUITO EMERGENCE

Mosquito larvae must live in water, whether it is a pond or a metal can full of water. In the United States, they are called "wrigglers." They hang upside down from the surface of the water, breathing air through a tube. Eventually, they turn into pupae, which stretch out on the surface when the adult is ready to emerge. The adult stretches upward until the ends of its long legs slip out of the pupa and its body can drop forward onto the surface film of the water (left). After resting for a short time, the mosquito flies away. Only the females suck blood – they need a meal of blood before they can lay their eggs. The males are nectar feeders.

SHY FROG

Adult frogs are very shy and leap into the water at the first sign of danger. Their long, streamlined shape and powerful back legs with webbed toes help them to swim fast. Frogs mate and lay their eggs in the water. The jelly around the eggs helps to keep them warm and protects the eggs from damage caused by other animals or the movement of the water. The eggs hatch into tiny tadpoles that have no legs and breathe through gills. Eventually, they develop into frogs, with legs and lungs, and hop out of the water onto land.

NEWT DANCE

In spring, the male great crested newt develops a high, ragged crest along his back and tail and turns orange-red underneath. He produces secretions from special glands to attract a mate. The female lays up to 300 eggs, which she wraps individually in the leaves of water plants. When seized, this newt secretes a nasty fluid.

EXTRA FOOD

Waterfowl, such as these swans, in towns and cities benefit from the extra food people bring for them. But they can also be harmed by polluted waters or injured by garbage, such as plastic bags and cans, or by fishing lines thrown away carelessly beside waterways. Swans sometimes die after becoming entangled in the lines or by swallowing the lead weights along with the stones they take in to help them grind up their food. The lead is ground up in its stomach and slowly poisons the swans. Nontoxic alternatives to lead weights and better riverbank behavior by fishermen have saved many swans from this unpleasant fate.

SPECIAL JOURNEYS

Changes in the food supply or seasonal changes in the weather may force some urban animals to embark on remarkable migration journeys. One record-breaking swallow flew from Johannesburg to Leninsk-Kuznetskiy in Russia, a distance of some 7,500 miles (12,000 km), in just 34 days. Other urban visitors, such as moose, wander over much smaller distances, but their journeys are also based on the need to find food.

The fruit bats of the tropics make regular mass migration journeys to find ripe fruit. Migrating animals find their way by using instinctive knowledge, physical landmarks, the Earth's magnetic field, sounds, smells, and the position of the sun, moon, and stars. It is ironic that feral pigeons have acquired such a high reputation for their homing skills since they find their home roost from relatively small distances – up to about 100 miles (160 km).

FRUITFUL SEARCH

Most fruit bats live in large colonies. In Kampala, Uganda, hundreds of thousands of bats hang from trees during the daytime. Fruit bats often migrate in search of ripening fruit. For instance, the grey-headed fruit bat of Australia moves about in search of wild figs. Australian flying foxes migrate periodically from Queensland to New South Wales, often doing considerable damage to fruit trees in northern and eastern Australia. Fruit bats also migrate to South Africa during the southern summer and fly northward along the Nile in the rainy season.

ROUTE CHANGES

People have radically changed the migration habits of the Canada goose, which used to breed in the Alaskan summer and fly south to the Gulf of Mexico for the winter. Now many geese remain in city parks all year round. Thousands of wintering geese also remain in wildlife refuges in the central U.S., rather than flying farther south. Geese can cause hygiene problems in parks because of the huge amount of waste they produce. A flock of 300 geese can produce a ton of waste in four days.

CAN SOMEONE TAKE MY ORDER?

This moose has obviously taken a liking to fast food! During the warmer seasons, moose follow a nomadic lifestyle, wandering over a vast expanse of country and sometimes ending up in cities. In the winter, they tend to collect together and retire to some sheltered area, where they remain until the warmer weather returns in spring. The promise of food may also draw them to cities in winter.

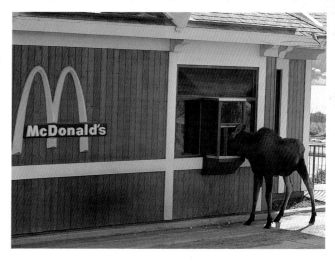

SOARING STORKS

White storks migrate from Europe into Africa to avoid the cold European winter, returning year after year to their favorite chimneys and rooftops to build their enormous nests. Migrating flocks of storks – sometimes hundreds strong – are a spectacular sight on their autumn migrations as they soar on the warm thermals rising over cities such as Istanbul and Gibraltar. They will not fly over large expanses of water where there are no thermals on which they can glide.

SWALLOW SURVIVAL

European swallows spend half the year in Europe and half the year in Africa. In the autumn, they leave behind the cold winter weather and the shortage of insect food and fly south to a relatively warm and safe environment in Africa. In spring, they fly north again to Europe, where there are long hours of daylight and an abundance of food – two advantages when rearing the young. On their migration journeys, swallows may cover as much as 186 miles (300 km) a day, at a speed of over 43 mph (70 km/h).

HITCHHIKERS

Some urban animals do not choose to make their journeys. They are accidentally carried around the world on ships or planes. This tree frog might very well find itself transported to a new home on a ship, as the bananas are shipped from a tropical country to a cooler one. Spiders are often transported like this, including the various "banana spiders," such as *Heteropoda venatoria*. Spiders also travel with bunches of grapes because they were busy feeding on grape pests when the grapes were harvested.

NESTS, EGGS, & YOUNG

PAPER NEST

Wasps build truly wonderful nests of papier-mâché made by the wasps themselves from chewed-up wood. The paper nest is made up of eight or more layers of six-sided cells that are joined to the layers above by pillars of paper. The queen wasp lays eggs in the cells that hatch into worker wasps. She has to glue the eggs into the cells to stop them from falling out. At the end of the summer, workers make larger "royal cells" in which to rear new queens. The whole nest is covered with several layers of wasp paper.

Birds, insects, frogs, toads, snakes, and mammals all find safe places to build their nests and raise their young in our homes, gardens, parks, and office blocks. The fact that some people put out food for town and city creatures is a real bonus for busy parents struggling to fill the ever-hungry mouths of their offspring. Birds, in particular, often choose the oddest spots for their nests, from old vacuum cleaners and empty paint cans to mail boxes and aircraft. A mallard duck even built her nest in a window box on the seventh floor of a block of apartments. She had to rely on a human helper to carry her ducklings down to the lake below. Urban birds make use of some unusual nesting materials, such as potato chip bags, plastic footballs, tennis rackets, and telephone wire. Wasps also build their nests in awkward places, such as porches, greenhouses, or even under beds.

UGLY DUCKLINGS

A housing development was built near the breeding grounds of this swan, so it now has to take its cygnets across pavement instead of grass to get to water. Mute swans usually have four to seven young grey cygnets, which cannot fly until they are four-and-a-half months old. In the Middle Ages swan meat, especially that of the fully grown cygnets, was highly prized as a source of food. Enormous numbers were eaten at royal banquets. At Christmas in 1251, Henry III of England collected 125 swans for the festive celebrations.

SNAKE INCUBATORS

Grass snakes often lay their eggs in garden compost heaps. The warmth given off by the rotting vegetation makes the heap into a natural incubator, which helps the embryos in the eggs to develop fast enough to survive their first winter. As well as compost heaps, grass snakes have been known to lay their eggs in manure heaps, piles of sawdust, and holes in the walls of bakeries, where the ovens keep the building very warm.

EGG CARRIER

The male midwife toad, found in western European gardens and quarries, is a particularly caring parent. He winds a string of 35–50 eggs around his back legs and carries them around for protection. He keeps the eggs moist by dipping them in shallow pools or puddles from time to time. After about three weeks, the male takes his eggy string to water, where they hatch into tadpoles and complete their development into adult toads.

PANT NEST

A pair of pants provides a handy nesting place for this wren, which has a brood of starving youngsters to feed. Birds that are willing to nest close to people can exploit nest sites that other competitors may not be bold enough to use. People may also help to deter some predators from attacking the nest and stealing the young.

ILLUMINATED NEST

This house sparrow has made its nest in a street lamp in Bahrain. Sparrows build untidy cupped or round nests of grass and straw lined with feathers. They will often rob other birds, such as pigeons or ducks, of their feathers. Hen sparrows lay four or five whitish eggs, often in other sparrows' nests. Two or three broods a year are normal, but four or five broods are possible. Eggs are incubated for about two weeks and the nestlings fledged in about another two weeks. Some young nestlings fall out of their nests onto pavements below before they are able to fly.

BLOWING BUBBLES

Froghoppers are bugs that suck the sap from plants. They get their name from the way the nymphs hop about like tiny frogs. Adults can fly away from danger, but nymphs cannot, so they protect themselves by living in blobs of white froth. The nymphs make the froth by blowing air into a sticky fluid that comes out of the rear end of the body. The froth also helps to stop the nymph from drying out.

DISCOVERING URBAN WILDLIFE

ROADSIDE PRESERVES

The grassy embankments at the side of roads can become useful mini-nature preserves if the grass and flowers are allowed to grow. This Texas roadside is filled with wild flowers that attract insects, and the insects, in turn, attract birds. Small mammals, such as mice and voles, can feed on seeds, roots, and shoots in these grassy areas. Although the animals have to put up with the traffic fumes and noise, they are not usually disturbed by people whizzing past in their cars, unaware of the living world so near their tires.

People have only been living in cities for some 5,000 years, so this is a relatively new habitat for wildlife. But, unlike other wildlife habitats, it is growing rapidly. By the year 2020, 80 percent of people will be living in towns and cities. We need to understand more about how urban animals survive if we are to encourage those animals that cause us no harm and control those that do. When we encourage urban animals to live in our towns and cities, it is inevitable that some of the popular species, such as butterflies and birds, will be eaten by unpopular ones, such as magpies and toads. This is all part of the balance of nature, even in an artificial urban setting. The four best ways to help urban animals are to provide shelter, homes, food, and water. Water is vital, both during summer droughts and winter frosts, and can be as small as a pan of water on a balcony or as large as a pond in a garden or city park.

BEE USEFUL

Some people in smaller towns manage to keep bees in their gardens. This beekeeper is checking on the well-being of the honeybees in one of his hives. Bees are excellent for gardens as they pollinate flowers while collecting nectar and pollen to feed their larvae. Back in the hive, they change the nectar into honey, which the beekeeper can harvest.

FREE FOOD

These rainbow lorikeets are feeding in a backyard in eastern Australia. People who feed birds in their gardens help them to survive and are rewarded by wonderful close-up views of the birds themselves. In countries colder than Australia, free food in the backyard or garden can be a real lifesaver in the winter, especially for small birds that need to eat a lot of food to keep warm.

CLEARING UP

Many areas of vacant land in cities, even small ones, can provide valuable habitats for wild animals, but only if unpolluted. These children are clearing up a wild patch of ground in London to make it safe for wildlife. Making things too neat and tidy both disturbs and discourages wild animals, though. Overgrown corners, with piles of old logs and stones, provide ideal places for animals to rest and hibernate. The greater the variety of native plants, including weeds, the greater the variety of insects and birds that can feed and shelter there.

FINDING OUT MORE

To plan the best conservation measures, it is important to know which animals are visiting our urban habitat, how many of them there are, and where they are living. Then any changes in populations can be recorded; problems avoided; and help given to animals where it is most needed. Information gathered by ordinary people identifying the birds on their streets and in their gardens can be very helpful to conservationists, although it is unnecessary, and harmful, to catch the birds! A pair of binoculars and a good bird book are all you need.

FEEDING BIRDS

If you do feed the birds, try to use a variety of different foods, such as peanuts, sunflower seeds, cheese, currants, bits of bacon rind, half coconuts, bread crusts, and cookie crumbs. You can offer food in a variety of ways – on a table for starlings, sparrows, and robins; in a hanging container for tits, woodpeckers, siskins and nuthatches; and on the ground for thrushes, dunnocks, and blackbirds. It is also a good idea to use a number of different places for the feeding stations. This makes it more difficult for cats to attack and gives the less aggressive birds a chance to feed. It also prevents the build-up of stale food, which might attract rats.

HERE ARE DIFFERENT TYPES OF BIRDFEEDERS YOU CAN MAKE YOURSELF.

1 Half a coconut
2 Peanuts or bird seed in a bottle or net
3 Peanuts hung on string or wire
4 Peanuts or fat in holes in a log
5 Pine cone filled with melted fat

URBAN TALES

CLEVER CROWS

Carrion crows living in Sendai City, Japan, have invented a clever way of cracking open the strong shells of walnuts. They wait until the traffic lights turn red, then fly down and place some nuts on the road. When the lights turn to green, the traffic rolls over the nuts and breaks them open. At the next red light, the crows hop quickly down to pick up the pieces of nut!

SUPER RATS

In some cities, there are as many rats as people, and so-called "super rats" have developed a resistance to some of the strongest poisons. In the mid 14th century, rat fleas were responsible for transmitting the Black Death, which killed a third of Europe's population.

CAMEL CLEANING

An unusual window cleaning firm in Cairo, Egypt, uses camels instead of people to clean the windows. A mixture of soap and sugar is put on the windows and the camels just lick the windows clean.

SNAKE STRIKES

An engineering company in Goa, India, was once closed down for three months by a large cobra that took up residence in the manager's office. Hindu workers felt that the sacred cobra should not be disturbed by loud factory noises and voted to wait for the snake to leave of its own accord. It was not in a hurry to leave.

SEWER CROCS

In 1935, an alligator over 6½ feet (2 meters) long was hauled out of a sewer onto a snowbank in upper Manhattan. No one knows where it came from. In the 1970s, unwanted pets were released into lakes, rivers, and sewer systems in the United States and the United Kingdom. Most of these died of the winter cold, but some survive to this day.

ELECTRIC MARTENS

Thousands of motorists in Winterthur, Switzerland, have suffered at the teeth of stone martens. Young animals have gnawed through ignition cables and cooling hoses inside their car engines, possibly seeing if they were edible. Martens in Austria managed to cause a power outage that lasted several days by tampering with the wires in a power station.

ACKNOWLEDGMENTS

We would like to thank: Helen Wire and Elizabeth Wiggans for their assistance. Artwork by Peter Bull Art Studio.
First edition for the United States, its territories and dependencies, Canada and the Philippine Republic, published 2000
by Barron's Educational Series, Inc.   Original edition copyright © 2000 ticktock Publishing Ltd.
U.S. edition copyright © 2000 by Barron's Educational Series, Inc.

250 Wireless Boulevard, Hauppauge, New York 11788 **http://www.barronseduc.com**
Library of Congress Catalog Card No. 99-68833   International Standard Book No. 0-7641-1077-2
Picture research by Image Select.   Printed in Hong Kong 9 8 7 6 5 4 3 2 1

Picture Credits: t=top, b=bottom, c=center, l=left, r=right, OFC=outside front cover, OBC=outside back cover, IFC=inside front cover

Bruce Coleman Collection; 8/9t, 10b, 11tr, 12/13c, 13b, 14l, 20/21t, 22ct, 24bl, 27tr. Chris Fairclough; 21bl. Heather Angel; 15br, 16/17b,
27bl, 30tl. Image Bank; 15t, 16cl & 32, 21br, 30bl. NHPA; OFC, 13r. Oxford Scientific Films; IFC, 2/3t, 2l & OFC, 3br, 3cr, 3t, 4bl, 4tl,
4/5b, 5tr, 5ct, 6l & OBC, 6br, 6/7t, 7tr, 7br, 9tr, 8bl, 9cl, 8tl, 9cr, 10tl, 10/11c, 11cr, 12tl, 14ct, 15c, 16tl, 17tr, 17cr, 17tl, 18/19c, 18/19t,
19c, 19tr, 20bl, 20br, 20tl, 22/23b, 23tr, 23cr, 23br, 24tl, 24/25b, 24/25c, 24/25t, 25br, 27cr, 26t, 26/27c, 29cl, 28bl, 28/29t, 29b, 28tl, 29cr,
29tr, 30/31t, 30br. Survival Anglia; 5tl. Tony Stone Images; 7cr, 18tl & OBC, 22l, 26l, 30cr.